FOUR GALAXIES

*Before each galaxy comes a black hole that
often tries to consume us and our happiness.*

A. NEWMAN

DEDICATION

To all the galaxies in the Universe and their blackholes.

CONTENTS

BLACK HOLE WUN

Galaxies are a system made of dark matter, dust, gas, and a million to trillion Stars. What holds them together is gravity. Just like the Earth, the beauty of these galaxies is marred by the black holes in their center.

Our first big bang experience took place during the 18th year of this life cycle. We were both still learning about life. The only difference was that they had more experience than us, so we just went with their flow.

There had been others before them, but none took control of the situation the way they did. There was just something about them that made them come off so confident. They were the type of being who took matters into their own hands rather than relying on others.

We were too afraid to do it ourselves. The opportunity to expand our life source had risen before, but for some reason, we would always fumble the ball. This time around, we attempted patience. Taking advantage of an opportunity when it comes, is the difference between being happy in life and just getting through it. We had broken things off a few weeks before our special night. Guess they had no one else to summon, but we were okay with being their booty appointment for the night. We didn't know how things would proceed, but as the children say, "We were down for anything!"

It was our first job interview as a creator of life. We were beyond nervous and equally excited. Our spider senses could feel what was about to take place, no questions asked on either side, and that's what built the anticipation.

They took control of the wheel, and we were just there for the ride. It happened so fast yet slow enough that we savored every moment of it. One minute, we were sitting in the entertainment room having small conversations about our day, then suddenly a few words led to their hands fondling around in our grey sweatpants.

It was surreal as we just watched them reach for our magic stick. "The royal tool is ready" that's what was going through our head as they proceeded to unwrap our tool. There was sweat around our collar because we weren't expecting this kind of royal treatment. All they were wearing was a shirt and a pair of red shorts, so they were eagerly pulled to the side.

Did we mention that red is our color? It just brings the beast out in us. Their super soaker was extremely wet, so we just slipped right in with no resistance. It was the first time we felt such a feeling, and the emotions coursing through us were like a high. Though we hadn't burned any broccoli recently, the rush was similar. It's been in someone's mouth before, and that was enjoyable too, but this feeling was different. It felt euphoric. We never wanted to leave.

Before we realized, it was over…way too soon, but we both enjoyed it. They decided from that night forward that we would get back together. Every chance we got, we engaged in this magical connection of two life forms. There were no questions asked. Our eyes would just connect, and BAM! Our limbs were entwined in passion. The ultimate show of affection any living being can receive or give.

At their request, "never pull out" was the only rule, which baffled us because usually, it's the other way around. However, we both enjoyed it too much not to end it inside, together. Of course, this comes with risks.

To create life from this act of nature between two living beings is a risk on its own. Though, whenever we were inside them, nothing else mattered. We went on strong for a few months together before the military life called us forward. Staying away from them wasn't something that we had imagined, but life happened, and we had to heed the call of duty.

Every week that went by during boot camp, all we could think about was them and their super soaker. Nine weeks total went by, and then it was finally time to graduate.

We were together again when they came to visit us for graduation, along with our Earth and sibling. Of course, we had to go back to the hotel for some alone time. We both were eager to explore each other again. It had been a long time since we enjoyed each other's body chemistry. In the back of our mind, we thought everything was fine but, it wasn't. That feeling we all get when something terrible is about to happen wouldn't go away.

One day, during our career training school, we decided to check their voice messages. Big mistake on our part! Turned out to be a terrible idea, but a necessary one. We heard someone else's voice. It sounded familiar, which brought back memories of past conversations about this familiar voice. The voice was telling our should have been first galaxy, to hurry up and get outside. They used to tell us that they were just a friend.

Their words, the other beings voice, kept replaying in our mind on a loop and it gave us the worst feeling. It felt like their words were burning a hole in our heart. We immediately started crying. How could they do this to us? We never knew that they could stoop to this level. We had plans for the future, but the past was already here before our present even had a chance to begin. The ride was over. There was no way forward because we had unintentionally taken a big step backward.

The energy we were starting to build had nowhere to go. Eventually, it imploded within itself and became the first blackhole in our heart.

PUREBRED 29

We were alone in the emptiness of space and time. We always wondered about the plain of existence without another soul to claim as our own. The Universe knows the right time and place to take action. However, lately, it felt like we were not even in an orbit.

If it wasn't for their Earth, we would've never met. Strange that they even wanted us to meet their creation, knowing our Taino flow was contagious. Though sometimes we wanted to stay away, they kept pulling us back in.

They set our future in motion with one simple notion of generosity. They shared pictures with us at work and even joked about dating their oldest, but they were already spoken for. Our connection was casual… simple. At least, that was the general vibe, but things were slowly setting into motion.

Their youngest was too young, but the middle one was just perfect. It almost didn't happen though. They had just finished high school and we were getting ready to go on our second tour downrange.

The first day we met, it felt like it came straight out of a scene from a love story. Things happened in slow motion because we didn't know what to do. It was almost like we were frozen in time. We were at work when they walked in, with what seemed to be birds and a slight breeze behind them. It felt like the Earth had stopped spinning. We can almost say it looked like butterflies were also flying around them, but that was just in our gut. Never in our lives had we seen such a beautiful angel. They were glowing, or perhaps, it was our imagination being filled with excitement.

We were so nervous, even before they approached us to say hello. When they started walking, we realized that it was in our direction, and that's when our heart started beating furiously. Once they made it over to our workstation, we froze. For the life of us, we couldn't say a single word. Their Earth was there watching, laughing at us because we were left so speechless like they knew it would happen this way. That's when we knew they were the one for us.

They were looking so much better in person. We didn't think they would find us attractive, but apparently, they did. They smiled and introduced themselves, and in that instant, we were over the moon. At that moment, there were no words to describe what we were feeling. Perhaps, euphoria. No, it was more than that.

Usually, we need to hear someone say their name a few times before our brain decides to remember it, but not theirs. It instantly drilled a spot in our brain and heart. The connection was so powerful that we hit it off right from the start. We went on several dates. Most of the time, their Earth asked us not to go back to the dorms together, but of course, that's where we always ended up. It would start slow and then heat up in a matter of seconds. That time spent together formed our love, which led to our nebula.

We should've fought harder to keep them, but we didn't think that something or anything would come from this collision. Like any good thing that starts, it has its end planned already.

They were sending us downrange again. Purebred-29's inner core was still in its beginning stages of life. The long distance between us would sever our love over time; that was a given. Things were going smooth for the first few months. We knew it was going to be hard, but we were committed.

We wrote letters to each other, an email in between. Thoughts started filling our heads with negative possibilities. Were they cheating on us or sneaking around the town in our own vehicle? It was indeed a possibility, but they were just assumptions. We could be wrong, but we could be right too. But that wasn't it. Being so far away was hard on both of us. Our minds would constantly fill with negative thoughts, and one thing would lead to another, increasing the strife between us.

Either way, we still pursued with the questioning. Of course, all accusations were denied. What did we think? That they were going to accept whatever we said? A highly unlikely scenario, but we just wanted to know the truth. A breakup is the only logical choice, and so it was decided. Our attempt to be done with each other was met with small sneaky links while seeing others. We came to realize that though we wanted to enjoy life, we just couldn't give up on each other.

Then came the time for us to move on to a new duty station, which changed everything. We were being blessed with a fresh start, around new living beings, new experiences. Things were looking up, and we were ready to embrace the flow. During our break from work before the move, we received a very unexpected call. It was Purebred-29, and they were expecting new life.

Immediately our first thoughts were,

"Wait, what?"

"How could this be? We haven't been together in months."

But then we recalled the goodbye kisses before we departed that turned into a quickie at the door that turned into a new life being formed. Our first nebula was coming into this world. How did we go from chasing another car down the road, waving a pistol out the window, to saying, "let's just get married?" It was all too much, and we didn't know how to handle it.

Now a whole new life was being started by us. The best thing to do was try to live for us. We had made up our mind, and we were going to see to it till the end. Things started off bad from the jump. We would constantly argue, sometimes when we were bored and other times over who was more boring. They didn't like being stuck at home all day while we worked to keep the roof up. Isn't that the way of things? At least, that's what we were taught. They didn't appreciate it, though. So, we fought some more, and things took a turn for the worst.

Once our bundle of joy came into this world, we thought things would change. After all, we had created a Star together. It felt like we were about to find our lost power, and that would allow us to handle the challenge life threw our way. Unfortunately, it didn't change a damn thing. We were both too immature for the life of raising another. The best thing we could do was separate, for both our sake.

Was it the right decision? No, which is something we agreed on. When the day finally came, we were both sad. Things were not supposed to end this way. All we could think about was how this would affect our Star. We were full of regrets, but the damage was done, and there were just some things that couldn't be taken back.

Our first galaxy was now becoming distant, with light years of darkness between us. We were left alone, in the vacuum of space.

Temptations were everywhere. Our sadness didn't last, but the emptiness was relevant.

Years have passed since we separated from Purebred-21. Our Star was becoming a Sun without us, and the saddest part was that we couldn't watch their transformation. Though, the love between us was still fueled by our spiritual connections.

BLACK HOLE TU

It wasn't the right time for us, we knew that, but the heart wants what the heart wants. Had it been a different timeline, we would be together to this day. We met unexpectedly through a mutual friend, but that's a story for our third eye to explain. We didn't keep anything from each other, so we kind of knew we were living on borrowed time. Isn't that how love is supposed to be? We understood our hearts belonged to someone else, but we moved forward anyway. Maybe that was the mistake we made.

When the day came that we had to part ways, the magical creation of life tried to keep us together, but it wasn't strong enough. Fingers were pointed in all directions, but neither could stay upset. It wasn't a matter of 'hearsay' but more of what our relationship had come to. We already knew we were living on borrowed time. Years would pass before we would speak again. Some things are better left broken.

Still, we tried to mend the hole like the song says, but it wasn't an option for us. Blackholes rarely close unless it explodes. Neither of us wanted beef, so chicken it was. In the end, we chose to forget about each other. We both moved on. We did check up on each other from a distance, but that was the extent of our connection. We were just glad to see them happy and prospering in life.

NEENEE 14

Who says opposites don't attract each other? In fact, sometimes, the difference in opinion brings us close together because it gives us a lot more to talk about.

Thanks to a mutual friend for linking our gravity fields together. It pulled us in like two dying Stars. We were in an adult toy store, which was interesting in its own merit. Just browsing stuff and trying to see if something catches our attention. They were shopping for a new toy to keep themselves occupied.

They grabbed one, and we joked about how it resembled our own tool in more ways than one. They weren't interested in our sexual jokes, though. It was our bad because that wasn't a line that would impress anyone. Truth be told, we were bragging about it.

They weren't looking for a Sun to fill their void at the time. They were more interested in another Earth to enter their solar system. "Greedy much?" We thought to ourselves, but it was cool though. Our mutual friend had already told us they were looking for a place to stay. We had extra space in our orbit for one more, so we offered it to them.

We got along great the first few months. For anyone, it would be hard to have a roommate of the opposite sex without having daydreams of each other, but surprisingly, it was great for us. It's not that we didn't encounter any temptations because we did, but somehow, we mastered our desires. We didn't want to overstep our boundaries, and we were damn sure that they wouldn't want us to come strong.

One day, while watching movies, we ended up licking lips and exchanging hip thrusts together. It all happened too soon, and we had no time to think about it all. The confusing part was, they were more attracted to the same sex, but we went along with the gravity that pulled us together. Sometimes, desires have no name, and they can manifest in anyone, so we didn't object to being their toy.

Why were we being allowed to taste this forbidden fruit? Though there were no complaints from this side, but there was this thought that was niggling in the back of our mind that something wasn't right. The only hiccup with this setup was our weak pull-out game. It was more non-existent than weak. Since this was new territory for us, things went pretty fast. First it was the couch, then the living room floor. We didn't expect this situation to go anywhere further than that. In all sense, this was just great sex between good friends.

One day we were sitting on that same couch with someone else, another Earth. Yes, things had progressed. We weren't the same person anymore. Life had changed in uncountable ways for us. Another day, another Earth… that's how we kept ourselves occupied.

Then here came Neenee-14 and the pregnancy stick with a plus sign on it. Our guest Earth asked if we were sleeping together.

"Yes" we replied.

"This date is clearly over," they proclaimed.

"Ah, yeah," were the only words we could muster up.

We were both left speechless, but obviously we both expected it eventually. No matter how shocking the news was, we never once thought about getting rid of it. It wasn't even an option. In the end, the confusion, panic and stress were overridden by the fact that there was a little life growing inside our Earth and one day soon, they would refer to us as their Sun.

So, we decided to allow this creation to occur. Months into the gases forming, we were notified that there were two nebulas in the mix. That panic, which we thought we had left behind, came back in full force

Two Stars were forming, and we didn't know what the future was going to look like. Not even in our wildest imaginations had it occurred to us that someday, we would be holding a new precious life in our arms. Now, that the nebula was multiplied; we had no words to express our feelings.

Tensions were building between our worlds. The guides of Neenee-14 tried to get involved, but we stood our ground. Why were they even angry with us? Weren't they supposed to be happy that a Sun so close to them was giving them another Star to hold and admire?

All this still remains a mystery to us. Life started anew when our twin Stars came into existence. There were some complications, some close calls, but they pulled through. Our friendship was damaged for the long run, but there was no reason we couldn't share the love for our creations. Call us the watcher of their existence, from a distance. We knew that things would never go back to the way they were before, but this wasn't something that we would ever wish to change. In the end, we knew that it was meant to be. The Creator never gives us more than we can handle.

BLACK HOLE TREY

It was around Christmas time when we met. Snow was falling and children were making snow creatures and snow angels. Also, it just so happened to be their Earth arrival day. We were happy to make their acquaintance. We danced together that night, even ended up kissing on our first night. To say it was magical would be an understatement. We were so happy that we couldn't stop laughing all night long, together. It was perhaps, one of the best days of our life.

Before we knew it, we were waking up next to each other every morning and saying goodnight. Slowly, unexpectedly, we fell in love. Was it written in faith? Perhaps, yes but we knew that this love was real.

They moved in without us even noticing. Well, we noticed but didn't mind. How could we? We now had someone to warm our bed and heart and it was a welcoming change from our otherwise lonely life. Things were just starting to get exciting.

Waking up next to them every morning was one of the greatest feelings we had felt in a long time. That even sounded good writing it down. Like all good things come to an end, so did this. The love they had for us was short lived. The morning sex, afternoon and coming-home-from-work sex, we miss that.

Every day, we ask ourselves, "Why didn't we try harder to keep what we had?"

Instead of making plans for our future, we accused them of sleeping around. When in reality, it was us who were sneaking out when they weren't looking. No, we weren't trying to get out of the relationship, but things just happened, and we had no control over it. Talk about self-destruction.

Things ended, but there was a new nebula inside of them forming. So, we had to change. We didn't know how to take it. This was a huge responsibility, and it was a part of us too. We couldn't even fathom leaving them behind. Were they really sneaking or not? Was the Star inside them ours? Should we have stuck around? There was no way of assuring ourselves. We just had to rely on our gut feeling.

We tried to be civil during the process, but there was too much tension. The fights were never ending and one of us would always try to point out that they were wrong. Nothing could hold us together.

Then the unexplainable happened. We were in the middle of a field exercise, so we couldn't accompany them in the hospital. Something was wrong with our little Star. There's nothing more worrisome than knowing that a life that isn't even born yet, one that we become attached to, is in danger and there was nothing we could do about it.

They blamed us for the darkness, and we blamed them. However, they were rightfully blaming us. Yes, it was our fault too but to put the entire blame on us…this wasn't how we had pictured things turning out.

Silence echoed heavily around us for months. Years have gone by and there is no sign of us still. The energy we were creating could've grown to be something amazing, but our inability to allow true happiness to form, prevented greatness. We were crying internally because we never thought that an end was a possibility.

YOSHEE 10

We were down range, fighting for the freedom of another nation when we met. It wasn't exactly the right time for hookups but when such things happen, who are we to question the wisdom of it all. While it was our third time around, it was their first.

At the same time, we were fighting our own negative vibes. They and their abusive significant other was just another part of life that we had to deal with. We were recently separated from ours. We found comfort in each other's company, even though we both knew it was a temporary fix…one that would lead to a lifetime of bickering back and forth.

Our time had come to part ways and head back to the homeland. They informed us there was a nebula forming, but the timing was not right, and it had to be eradicated. This brought back the past and we didn't have the energy to go through it all again, so we bid goodbye. Our friendship stayed intact though.

A few years would go by that we lost contact. For some crazy reason, the Universe wanted us to have another shot at it. They say that when someone is meant for a person, the world works in mysterious ways to bring them together. We linked up for a wild weekend with friends. One night with Yoshee-10 became a morning of waking up not remembering what had taken place. All we could remember is that we had partied hard and grown folk things had gone down with them. We did hookup but what happened was hazy in our mind. Then it resulted in yet another nebula forming. This time, we decided to let it grow. We were fully invested, and we knew that we were ready 100%. It was a new Star in this new galaxy we were creating.

The timing still wasn't right, but we continued anyways. At first, we questioned whether the nebula was of our own seed. We attended the shower together with no hiccups. Our excitement was beyond words, and they too had the same feeling… or so we thought.

We were welcomed into their orbit, but clearly there was some animosity that no one cared to express. We brushed it off and pushed forward. It all seemed fine in the beginning, and we didn't want to rock the boat. We never asserted our rights. Yes, we were responsible for the nebula too, but we didn't want them to feel smothered.

As a friend, we accompanied them in the hospital for the arrival of our new creation. The thought of if it was ours remained, but we took it one day at a time, just in case. The day we found out the truth that this new Star was indeed ours, we were ecstatic but also a little curious as to where this path would lead. This time, the nebula would become a Star and we were eager to watch them grow.

The distance between the Earth and Sun grew over time. We weren't in control of it. As they moved on, so did we. They no longer wanted us to be part of our Star's lifespan, but we begged to oppose that notion. We argued with them that a Star needs a Sun and Earth to flourish. With just one, they might fall to the Earth and get shattered. We couldn't even think about what would happen if we had no influence in their life. We fought hard and, in the end, we prevailed to remain in their life. It was a sweet victory.

BLACK HOLE FORTH

Creating life is one of the greatest abilities we as living beings poses. It's one of those miracles that we have been in awe of since the beginning of time. Sometimes, things go wrong, or the timing isn't right. We don't talk about it anymore. All we say to ourselves is, "We did our best."

It was too soon after our first Star was created. We waited the allotted amount of time between building new worlds. Somehow our fertile Earth took the seed on the first try.

"This is it," we said in our mind. We had to prepare ourselves because this was really happening. We were both in shock, but we were also not ready for another so soon. It was a difficult decision that had to be made. Sitting at the clinic of deceased energy souls, the goosebumps were nonstop. It was silent the whole time there. Our nerves on edge because what we were about to do, was not something that we had ever planned. But life happened and we had to choose. We weren't in the right mind or at a position in life where this could work out for us.

Afterwards, no words were spoken. We saw a glass angel at the store that stood out to us, so we purchased it, as a remembrance of the nebula that was lost. On display it went over the fireplace, as a reminder of the blackhole we decisively created. It was yet another void but this one had been created by our choices. Gone but not forgotten…that was what we thought. Our nebula was an energy that would remain forever.

KEYU 21

Before we knew it, it was time to explore our final life destination through the cosmos. We spent what seemed like eternities searching for love, just to have love find us, unexpectedly! The euphoria of it was unexplainable. We couldn't put into words the emotions we were feeling.

To think we had been through three already, we were a little afraid to think about or face what the world had in store for us. Never would we have imagined a fourth. There are still many living beings, who we know, that haven't even experienced the happiness of a first and here we were. What baffled us was that never in our wildest imaginations had we pictured that the fourth would be okay with there being a previous three.

The distance between us was immense at first and that was expected. We weren't familiar with them, and neither were they with us. Somehow, the negative energy surrounding our lives gave way for a path to one another and we found ourselves holding hands. The Yin to the Yang became one without either of us even trying.

Never in our life had we raised our hands and prayed to The Creator to shine their light upon us, but it seemed like they had listened to the voice in our heart and made sure that we receive the happiness that we deserved.

Before our galaxies collided, they were living the simple life. Not that this life was going any smoother for us, but destiny must have had a hand in our meeting the way we did because things were starting to look up for us. We wouldn't call it a twin flame story, but this is kind of like a twin flame story. Yes, we are talking in circles, but it is what it is.

We needed some extra cash on the side, so we applied to be the topflight security of the local movie theater in town. The same movie theater Keyu-21 happened to be making a living at. We knew that things were tight in the moment so we wanted to make sure that we wouldn't be tethered by low cash.

Every day, the crowd swallowed them whole and since we weren't working where they were positioned, we never saw even a glimpse of each other. It wasn't until a couple a weeks later that we came across in the hall.

When their energy was first detected by our radar, our jaw dropped.

"Who is that?" we asked a coworker.

"Oh no! Stay away from that one." they proclaimed.

This made us want them even more. We approached with strategic caution, like a lion approaching its next meal. The excitement of it all was making us feel hot. Of course, our initial advances were met with resistance. It was more like, they ignored us completely. We didn't mind though because that's how games proceed. We exchanged smiles for a while, barely said hello to each other and that was it. It seemed like they were not interested but the vibe told us different.

One day, we were caught off guard. There we were, doing our job, securing the scene. Well actually, we were enjoying a few minutes of the movie that was playing. Our attention was on making sure the guests were behaving. Thinking no one was behind us, we dug into our pants to pull our boxers out of our ass and that was the moment we heard a melodic voice behind us. It was so embarrassing!

"So, this is what they pay us to do now, pick wedgies out our ass?" Keyu-21 said to break the ice.

We couldn't help but laugh together, for the first time. Despite the humiliating situation we were caught in, we were glad they chose to diffuse the moment with a joke. We thought that now for sure they would show their interest in us.

However, even after our first encounter, they refused to give us their digits so we could reach them after hours. Though the fiery looks that we exchanged in the theatre were off the charts, there was no action later. We took the next step and asked their roommate for the numbers, on the low.

It started as just "What are we doing" texts. That later turned into our first meal together which was at this fancy restaurant we both loved at the time. These days, it's not considered fancy, but still one of our favorites, as it has our memories.

Most of the time when two beings meet and feel a connection, they embark in the act of love making, not us though. Then there is the three-date rule, which if it was the case, we would have been glad.

But they pulled the 90-day card out on us.

"No cookie for 90 days" they proclaimed.

We have never been put in such a situation where we had to wait for the goodies. Confused and not sure how to respond, we agreed. It was the longest 90 days ever, but in the end, it was worth it. The anticipation kept building and when the time came to explode, both our world's sheeted white with pleasure.

Out of all the other worlds we stumbled upon during our journey in life, never have we felt so wanted and needed. The feelings were mutual. Together we would create beautiful life. Like any relationship, there were heated moments, but we always managed to send ourselves into hyper drive and push through the meteor belts that tried to stop us from becoming a unit. When a bond forms that is larger than life, we have to make sure that we see it to the end and that's what we had in our mind. We wanted to pass all obstacles and reach that bliss that happy couples talked about.

Being responsible for not one but four galaxies may seem like a life full of stress, but it really isn't. The joy of having so much to give and receiving it tenfold is something one can only dream of and yet, we achieved it. The ability to juggle four balls only takes time and patience and strong will power. Not that we are saying we had them all, but we managed to learn and that's what counts. Though patience is the key to it all, as it helps us wake up every morning and face the day with vigor. Having someone who is willing to assist and push us to uphold our responsibilities also helps. They are like the guiding light that keeps shining and even when they do dim, they keep us company with their presence.

That one scene of our first shared laugh, turned into decades of togetherness and the creation of two beautiful Stars that shine over our horizon. Together we will forever be a unity.